Mount Rundle, Banff National Park.

The CANADIAN ROCKIES

The Three Sisters is a landmark in the Canmore area.

THE CANADIAN ROCKIES

Banff Avenue with Cascade Mountain in the background

The "Shining Mountains"

The Canadian Rockies contain some of the most dramatic mountain scenery in the world! And all of it was once under water!

Although the Rocky Mountain chain extends from the Yukon Territories south to the Mexican border, the highest most spectacular peaks occur in Canada north of Vancouver. Today our Canadian Rockies, together with the more rounded peaks belonging to our southern neighbours, still remain rugged, unspoiled and little inhabited.

For at least 11,000 years, and perhaps many thousands more, Indian tribes called the "Shining Mountains" theirs. The name given by the Indians was recorded by the Verendrye brothers who came from France in 1742 to "discover" an area of the mountains in present-day Montana.

In the early 1700's, explorers returning from the North American continent mentioned an Indian people living in a country 'with fabled peaks reaching up to the sky!' The name "Rockies" seems to have been given first in French by an explorer called Leguardeur St. Pierre in 1752. In his diary, he aptly named them "Montagnes de Roches" (Mountains of Rock).

THE CANADIAN ROCKIES

A Never-Ending Journey!

Before the CPR railroad opened up transportation, it took weeks of arduous trekking on foot or horseback to cross them, in most cases, blazing your own trail as you went, and confronting both wild animals and surprised natives en route! The early explorers probably thought that the north-south chain of mountains would not be too wide and that there would be welcoming plains waiting on the far side. Such thinking probably kept them going!

Today's traveller heading west from the prairies may well believe that there is only one range of mountains to cross before reaching the Pacific Coast. The Rockies chain is the first of seven major north-south ranges separating the prairies from the Pacific Ocean.

Still, the Rockies are the most grandiose and awe-inspiring of the seven chains. Because Arctic air currents flow south over the Rockies between October and April, repelling the moist warmer air mass moving east from the Pacific, the Rockies' colder climate has attracted fewer inhabitants than the Pacific Coastal mountains. Thus they have remained relatively uninhabited.

The Mountains Rise Up

It took a mere 50 million years for the Rockies to form! The process actually began 600 million years ago in the late Precambrian when the western part of the continent, now Alberta and British Columbia, was totally submerged in a shallow sea. Over 500 million years, much sediment built up in this giant inland sea.

Two tectonic plates, that of the westward-pushing Canadian Shield and that of the eastward-pushing Pacific plate came together and began to push upward, so that land which had been under water was gradually forced upwards to form the mountains we know to-day.

Volcanic activity continued to shape the mountains until a "recent" ice age only 12,000 years ago gave the Rockies their "modern" shape with our familiar rivers and icefields.

Mineral Riches

The debris left behind from the slow upward shifting of the two continental plates contained fossil-rich marine sediments left over from the inland sea. The Rockies are also laden with ore of all kinds, especially gold, copper and silver, not to mention jade and more humble but important substances like coal. The quest for this mineral wealth continues to inspire many daring adventurers.

How the National Parks Began

Many square miles of the Canadian Rockies are now national parks or special forest reserves. People may not purchase land in the parks; however Parks Canada leases the land within town sites such as Banff and Jasper. The story behind the founding of Canada's first national park is interesting. Three railroad workers, Thomas and William McCardell and their friend Frank McCabe, were exploring, intrigued by a strangely warm area in the Banff vicinity, now well-known as the Cave and Basin outside Banff, when they spotted steam issuing from a cleft in the rock. The water down below was also incredibly warm and there was a heavy sulphurous smell in the air.

These adventurers clambered down into a

hot pool which can be seen to-day just as it was in 1885. They had a marvellous bath and came up feeling incredibly relaxed yet exhilarated!

Tourist Attraction

The three saw the potential and began bringing small groups of workers to the seductive spot. They tried to lay claim to their discovery only to have the grass cut from under their feet by the ambitious railroad president, Sir William Van Horne. He instantly realized that the "Magic Waters", long known as such to the Indians, could be a superb tourist attraction! "Since we can't export the scenery, we'll have to import the tourists!" he quipped, and proceeded to do just that, building a vast and incredibly elegant hotel, the Banff Springs Hotel, in the midst of dense wilderness! This hotel was only the first in a chain of hotels undertaken by Van Horne. A 10 square mile federal reserve, forerunner of Canada's first National Parks, was built around the springs. Two years later, a slightly larger area, 260 square miles, Rocky Mountain National Park, was set aside. The total size of Banff National Park today: 2,564 square miles (4,126 square kilometers).

And what about the intrepid discoverers of the springs who deserved the real credit? Surely they were richly rewarded for such a find? Van Horne convinced the Canadian government to step in and refuse their claim in his favour, buying them off with a paltry $900, and ...the having rights to a small adjacent area! The poor men protested, but to no avail.

People From Everywhere

Once the national parks came into being,

along with the completion of the Canadian Pacific Railroad across Canada, people began arriving from many foreign lands. Some of the first were Swiss mountain climbers, who came out with the new railroad and began guiding other visitors. Many of them stayed to form the growing present-day community of third and fourth generation Swiss settlers in Western Canada.

Well-to-do Americans and European aristocrats were also lured by the elegant new Banff Springs Hotel completed in 1888, which contrasted dramatically with the untamed wilderness around it. At night, the brightly lit hotel with the surrounding forest resembles a great passenger ship on a dark sea.

A group of Yale University students were the first to climb above 11,000 feet in the Canadian Rockies. The Yale-Lake Louise Club climbed Mount Temple in 1894.

Then came a series of daring mountaineers, not only Swiss, but Austrian, British and North American. The Columbia Icefield was discovered in 1898 by two British climbers, Collie and Woolley.

In the "early" days before World War II, hiking or hunting in the Rockies was a true wilderness experience; according to renowned outfitter and writer, Andy Russell, people would be out on the trail with reliable guides for weeks on end and never smell civilization! Nowadays, people enter the Rockies at relatively high speed and "do" the excursions in a matter of hours or a few days at most, in keeping with to-day's accelerated life style.

A Refuge From Civilization

While things aren't as pristine as they were

100 years ago, despite increasing numbers of visitors and local residents, the Rockies are still surprisingly clean! Everywhere on the hiking trails are large signs: "Pack out your garbage"! Somehow even the least respectful kind of people make an effort at this, perhaps because they sense the wonder of the place, unlike any other corner of North America in its grandiose beauty.

Nowadays, the Rockies' charm has become legendary throughout the world. Tourists come from the Far East, Japan and Hong Kong, from all over Europe and South America, Australia, etc., to enjoy the comfort of four and five-star hotels and the relatively unspoiled sights set up for tourists. Nonetheless, people who want to rough it, packing in their food and gear, can still do it all on foot and disappear from civilization for days and weeks on end, blissfully catching their own fish for dinner and eating berries for dessert to enjoy a feeling of "discovery" and elation similar to that of the early explorers.

Birds & Beasts, Flowers and Fossils!

Plant and animal varieties are in the hundreds in the Rockies. Visitors are not permitted to pick flowers lest they should become extinct, nor are they allowed to remove any undersea fossils they might find atop mountain peaks. Hunting is also forbidden in order to protect certain game which is already in decreasing supply. Constant pressure exists to develop the more accessible wilderness areas within the Parks. Yet it is the pristine untouched nature of the Rockies which attracts visitors, and the variety of life forms found there.

There are elk, deer, moose and big horn sheep always appearing to perch precariously out on a ledge, rabbits, hare, funny little pikas, looking like an out-of-focus rabbit, pristine white mountain goats, coyotes, beaver, many kinds of squirrel, wildcats and cougars, and most awesome of all Rocky mountain beasts, the grizzly bear. Elk and other horned animals when provoked can be menacing but the bear family, both brown and grizzly, are perhaps the only major threat to human beings, especially when hikers inadvertently get in between a mother and her cubs. While the grizzly is larger, weighing up to 800 lbs. as opposed to the 500 lb. maximum of the black bear, probably the black bear is more dangerous to humans because they are more likely to explore close to campsites and trails than the aloof grizzly. "Black" bears can in fact be sandy blond in colour, while grizzlies are usually dark brown; but they too may be blond occasionally!

Being There

Words and pictures can only give an impression of a beauty that defies description: hiking in the sharp, clean air, testing your body as you push yourself up steeper and steeper grades in search of the highest peak, and the accompanying feeling of exhilaration when you look out over a panorama of snow-capped peaks in front and below, the smell of new plants and warming earth emerging from winter, standing motionless watching a moose splashing through water, these things will reveal the real spirit of the "Shining Mountains". This book is a memento of those experiences.

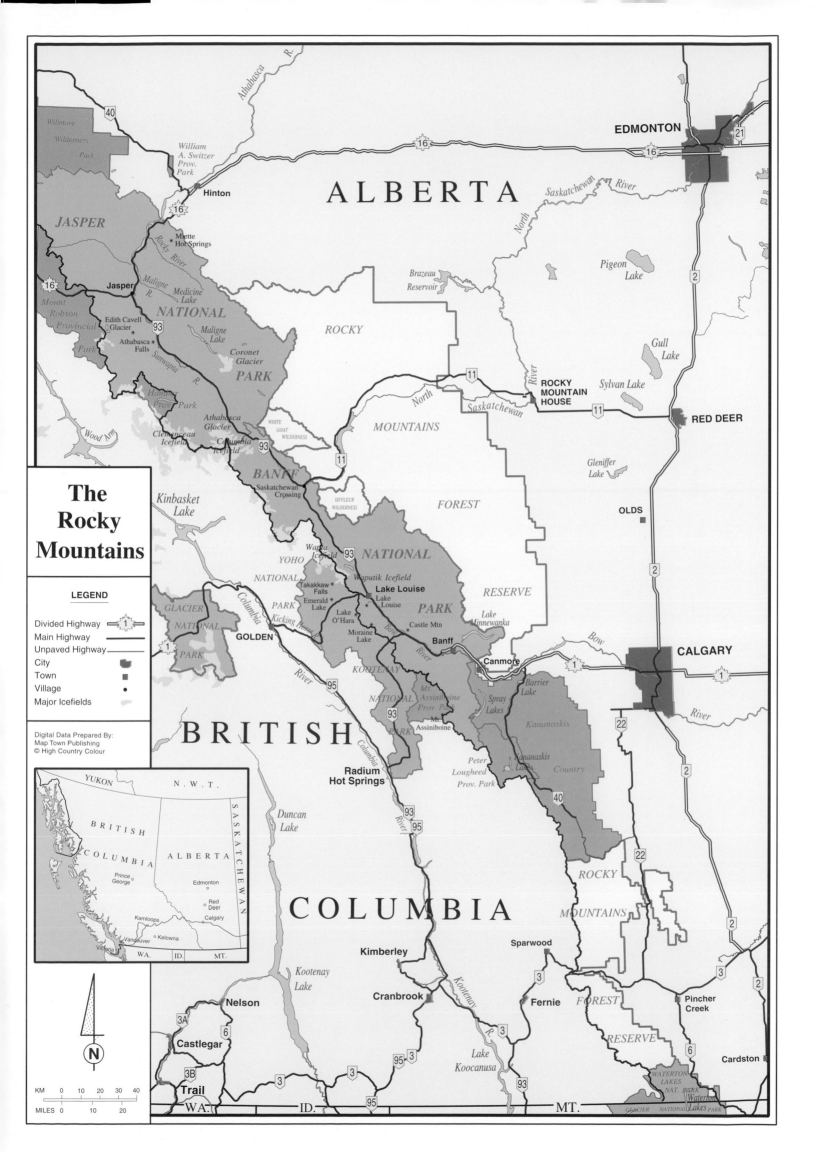

The Rocky Mountains

LEGEND

Divided Highway
Main Highway
Unpaved Highway
City
Town
Village
Major Icefields

Digital Data Prepared By:
Map Town Publishing
© High Country Colour

ALBERTA

EDMONTON

Hinton

JASPER

Mette Hot Springs

Jasper

William A. Switzer Prov. Park

Willmore Wilderness Park

Mount Robson Provincial Park

Edith Cavell Glacier

Athabasca Falls

NATIONAL

Medicine Lake

Maligne Lake

Coronet Glacier

PARK

Hamber Prov. Park

Clemenceau Icefield

Athabasca Glacier

Columbia Icefield

WHITE GOAT WILDERNESS

Saskatchewan Crossing

BANFF

Kinbasket Lake

Wood Arm

SIFFLEUR WILDERNESS

Wapta Icefield

YOHO

NATIONAL

PARK

Takakkaw Falls

Emerald Lake

Waputik Icefield

Lake Louise

Lake Louise

Lake O'Hara

GLACIER

NATIONAL

PARK

GOLDEN

Moraine Lake

Castle Mtn

Banff

NATIONAL

PARK

RESERVE

Lake Minnewanka

Canmore

KOOTENAY

Mt. Assiniboine Prov. Park

Mt. Assiniboine

Barrier Lake

Spray Lakes

Kananaskis

CALGARY

NATIONAL

PARK

Radium Hot Springs

Peter Lougheed Prov. Park

Kananaskis Lakes

Kananaskis Country

ROCKY

MOUNTAINS

FOREST

RESERVE

ROCKY

MOUNTAIN

HOUSE

RED DEER

OLDS

Pigeon Lake

Gull Lake

Sylvan Lake

Gleniffer Lake

Athabasca R.

Rocky River

Maligne R.

Sunwapta R.

Columbia River

Kicking Horse

Bow River

North Saskatchewan River

Saskatchewan River

Duncan Lake

Kootenay Lake

Nelson

Castlegar

Trail

Kimberley

Cranbrook

Radium Hot Springs

Sparwood

Fernie

Lake Koocanusa

Kootenay R.

Pincher Creek

Cardston

WATERTON LAKES NAT. PARK

Waterton Lakes Park

GLACIER NATIONAL PARK

FOREST

RESERVE

BRITISH

COLUMBIA

YUKON

N.W.T.

BRITISH

COLUMBIA

ALBERTA

SASKATCHEWAN

Prince George

Edmonton

Red Deer

Kamloops

Calgary

Kelowna

Vancouver

Victoria

WA.

ID.

MT.

KM 0 10 20 30 40
MILES 0 10 20

N

WA.   ID.   MT.

Previous page: The chateau at Lake Louise overlooks one of the
most famous views in the Rockies. Above: The Banff Springs Hotel
and Bow Valley.

The flower gardens at the Banff Administration Building with
Mt. Cascade in the background.

The entrance to the Chateau Lake Louise.

Winter at Lake Louise, and the Victoria Glacier.

The Cave and Basin.

Mt. Assiniboine, one of the most unique mountains in the
Rockies 11870 ft. (3618 m).

The Banff Springs Hotel.

The Upper and Lower Waterfowl Lakes.

Crowfoot Glacier is one of the many glaciers visible from the
Icefield Parkway.

Natural Bridge in Yoho National Park.

Lake O'Hara in Yoho National Park.

Winter is slow to leave the high alpine areas of the Canadian
Rockies.

These giant machines transport visitors out on the glacier for a first hand look at the massive Icefield.

The Athabasca Glacier, one of very few glaciers accessible by road.

Previous page: Snow coaches tour the immense Athabasca Glacier.
Above: Wapiti, commonly known as the elk.

Takakkaw Falls is the highest waterfall in Canada (380 m).

Emerald Lake is a popular stop for visitors to Yoho National Park.

Mt. Robson, the highest peak in the Canadian Rockies at 12972 ft. (3954 m) is one of the great peaks of the world. The Indians named the peak "The Mountain of the Spiral Road" (Yuh-hai-has-kun).

Lower terminal of the Jasper Tramway.

The Jasper Tramway lifts visitors to the summit of the Whistlers
for spectacular views of the area.

Roger's Pass in Glacier National Park.

The spectacular view from Sulphur Mountain.

Gondola cars at Lake Louise

Lake Louise in full bloom.

Hector Lake.

The Crossing is one of the largest service centres along the Parkway.

The Rockies come alive with colour as flowers arrive in the spring.

Amethyst lake, found at the foot of the Ramparts in the Tonquin Valley.

(Top) The Banff Springs Hotel
(Bottom) The Club House at the Banff Springs Golf Course.

Previous page: The Banff Springs Hotel opened in 1888.

Banff Avenue.

The view point at Roger's Pass.

Lake Louise.

Previous page: Peyto Lake
Lake Louise nestled below Mt. Victoria.

Cascade Mountain stands tall above Banff.

Nigel Creek Viewpoint.

Nigel Creek Falls.

Johnston Canyon.

Erosion in the Canadian Rockies has created many interesting sites to visit such as this rock arch at Johnston Canyon.

Icefield Snowcoach.

Storms appear quickly over the Athabasca Glacier.

Previous page: Maligne Lake and Spirit Island, Jasper National Park.
Above: Lake Minnewanka.

Castle Mountain is the most distinctive
peak between Banff and Lake Louise.

During the short summer period in the Rockies, a host of wild
flower species come into bloom.

Mt. Rundle.

Banff townsite with Mt. Rundle in the background.

Twin Falls in Yoho National Park.

View of Jasper townsite from the Tramway.

Jasper the Bear welcomes all visitors to his friendly town.

Headwaters of the Bow River; The Wapta Icefield melts into
the deep turquoise waters of Bow Lake.

Winter At Lake O Hara, Yoho National Park.

Renowned in the Rockies, the Big Horn Sheep.

Wildlife in the Rockies are sometime overcome by their curiosity.

Grizzly Bear.

(Wapiti) Elk.

Previous page: The Banff Springs Hotel and Bow Valley.
Above: White-tailed deer.

Banff National Park Administration Building.

Vermilion Lakes, looking towards Mt. Rundle.

The Cave and Basin on Sulphur Mountain.

Tangle Creek, along the Icefield Parkway.

Sunwapta Falls, Jasper National Park.

Previous page: The Chateau Lake Louise.
Above: Moraine Lake in the Valley of the Ten Peaks.

Pyramid Mountain, Jasper National Park.

Previous page: View of Banff and area from Sulphur Mountain.
Above: Mt. Edith Cavell in Jasper National Park.

The Columbia Icefields.

Previous page: The Columbia Icefield is an area of exceptional
mountain scenery.
Above: Moraine Lake in the Valley of the Ten Peaks.

Tonquin Valley, Jasper National Park.

Jasper Park Lodge.

The Prince of Wales Hotel in Waterton Lakes.

Pyramid Lake, Jasper National Park.

Mt. Victoria at Lake Louise.

Published and Distributed by:
HIGH COUNTRY COLOUR LTD
1909 10th Avenue S.W.
Calgary, Alberta, Canada
T3C 0K3

(403) 244 - 3511
http://www.hccolour.com

Written by:
Action Communications Int'l

Edited by:
Don Jenkins

Design by:
Brad Nickason
Don Jenkins

Photography by:
Henry Beckmann
C P Archives
Bob Hart
Bob Herger
High Country Colour
Simon Hoyle
Don Jenkins
Lyle Korytar
Angus McNee
Bo Semeniuk

Canadian Cataloguing in Publication Data
ISBN 0-920573-22-3   English edition

Copyright © 1989 High Country Colour
Fifth (Revised) Edition 1998
Ninth Printing 1998

Produced in Canada
Printed in Singapore